JOUF

MW00783136

Play Along with 8 Great-Sounding Tracks

BOOK & PLAY-ALONG CDs
WITH TONE 'N' TEMPO CHANGER

About the TNT Changer

Use the TNT software to change keys, loop playback, and mute tracks for play-along. For complete instructions, see the **TnT ReadMe.pdf** file on your enhanced CDs.

Windows users: insert a CD into your computer, double-click on My Computer, right-click on your CD drive icon, and select Explore to locate the file.

Mac users: insert a CD into your computer and double-click on the CD icon on your desktop to locate the file.

Recordings produced and mixed by Doug Emery, Lee Levin, and Dan Warner
Guitars and bass: Dan Warner
Keyboards: Doug Emery
Drums and percussion: Lee Levin

Cover photo: © Ross Halfin

Produced by
Alfred Music Publishing Co., Inc.
P.O. Box 10003
Van Nuys, CA 91410-0003
alfred.com

Printed in USA.

ISBN-10: 0-7390-7427-X (Book & 2 CDs)
ISBN-13: 978-0-7390-7427-5 (Book & 2 CDs)

Alfred

Contents

Drum Charts*

* For your convenience, printable PDF versions of the drum charts are included on the enhanced CDs.

DON'T STOP BELIEVIN'

Words and Music by
JONATHAN CAIN, NEAL SCHON
and STEVE PERRY

Verses 1 & 2:

1. Just a small town girl,___ liv- in' in a lone- ly world.___
2. Just a cit- y boy,___ born and raised in South De- troit,___

She took the mid-night train__ go- in' an- y - where.___
He took the mid-night train__ go- in' an- y - where.___

Interlude:

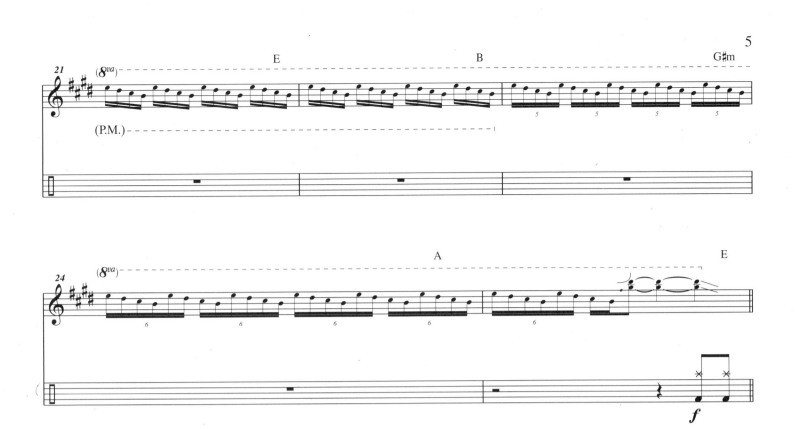

Verse 3:

A sing-er in a smok-y room.__ The smell of wine and cheap per-fume.__

For a smile_ they can share the night;_ it goes on and on__ and on__ and on.__

Bridge:

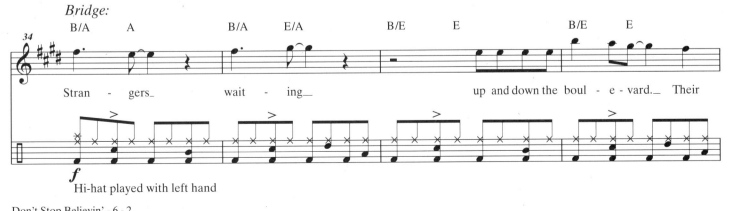

Stran - gers_ wait - ing__ up and down the boul - e - vard.__ Their

Hi-hat played with left hand

6

shad - ows__ search - ing__ in the night.___

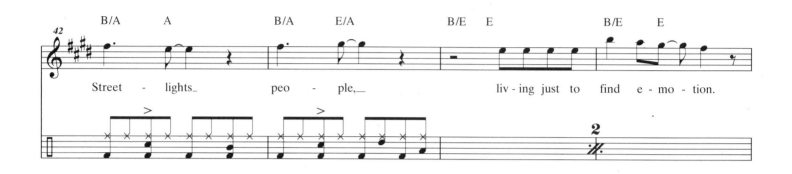

Street - lights__ peo - ple,__ liv - ing just to find e - mo - tion.

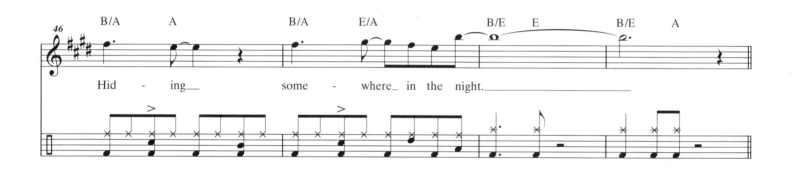

Hid - ing__ some - where__ in the night.___

Interlude:

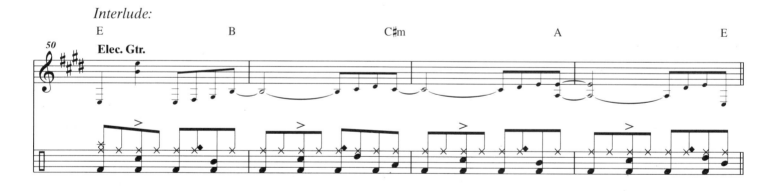

Verse 4:

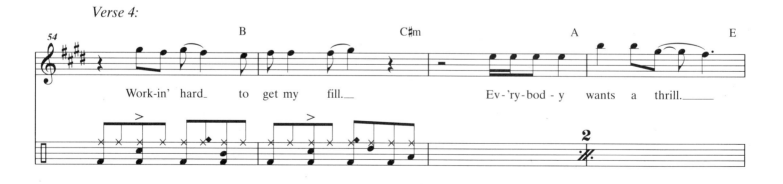

Work-in' hard__ to get my fill.__ Ev-'ry-bod - y wants a thrill.___

Don't Stop Believin' - 6 - 3

Verse 5:

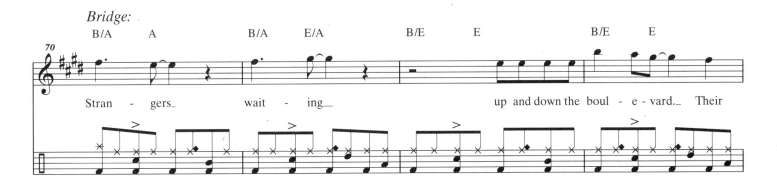

Bridge:

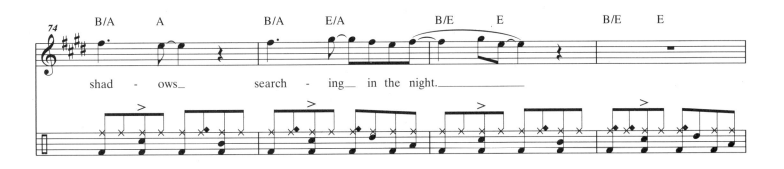

8

FAITHFULLY

Words and Music by
JONATHAN CAIN

Moderately slow ♩ = 66

Faithfully - 4 - 1

Faithfully - 4 - 4

LIGHTS

Words and Music by
NEAL SCHON and STEVE PERRY

Verse:

Chorus:

LOVIN', TOUCHIN', SQUEEZIN'

Words and Music by
NEAL SCHON and STEVE PERRY

Moderately slow ♩. = 69

Intro:

Lovin', Touchin', Squeezin' - 6 - 1

Verse 2:

Chorus:

Outro:

OPEN ARMS

Words and Music by
JONATHAN CAIN and STEVE PERRY

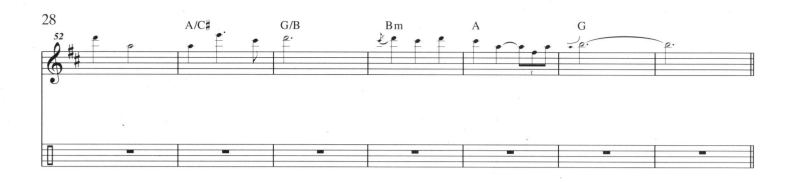

Verse 2:

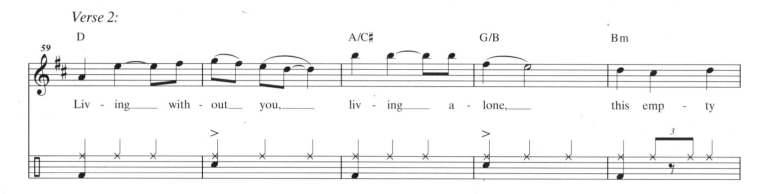

Liv - ing____ with - out____ you,____ liv - ing____ a - lone,____ this emp - ty

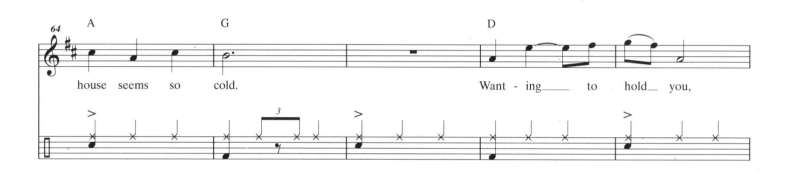

house seems so cold.   Want - ing____ to hold____ you,

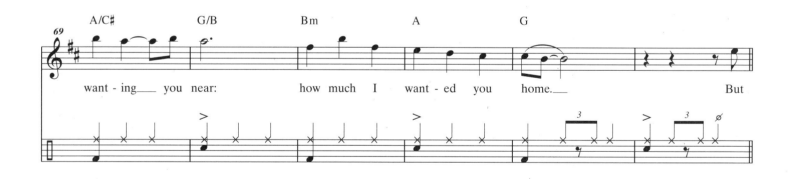

want - ing____ you near: how much I want - ed you home.____   But

Pre-chorus:

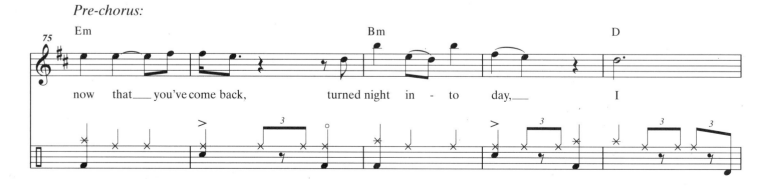

now that____ you've come back,   turned night in - to day,____   I

Chorus:

SEND HER MY LOVE

Words and Music by
JONATHAN CAIN and STEVE PERRY

It's been___ so___ long_____ since I've seen___ her___ face.___

You___ say she's do - in' fine.___

Send Her My Love - 5 - 1

32

Verse 2:

Outro:

Send___ her, send___ her my___ love;___

ros - es nev - er fade.___

Mem - o - ries___ re - main;___

send___ her, send___ her my___ love.___

Freely

Elec. Gtr.

SEPARATE WAYS
(WORLDS APART)

Words and Music by
JONATHAN CAIN and STEVE PERRY

Moderately ♩ = 132

Separate Ways (Worlds Apart) - 8 - 1

Verse 2:

Chorus:

88
Am7 Bm7 Cmaj9
___ my love; miss___ you, love.___

91
Em D
Some - day love___ will find___ you. Break those chains that bind___ you.___

95
Cmaj7 Am7
One night will___ re - mind___ you how we touched___ and went___

98
D5 D#5 Em
___ our sep - 'rate ways. If he ev - er hurts___ you,

101
D Cmaj7
true love won't___ de - sert___ you.___ You know I___

104
Am7 D5 D#5
___ still love___ you though we touched___ and went___ our sep - 'rate ways.

Guitar Solo:

WHO'S CRYING NOW

Words and Music by
JONATHAN CAIN and STEVE PERRY

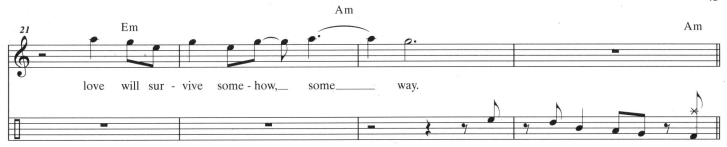

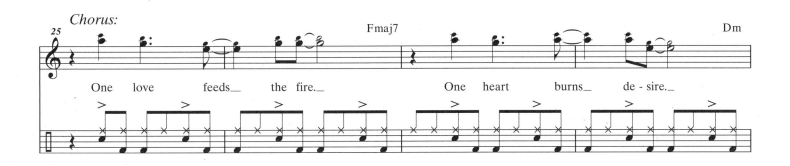

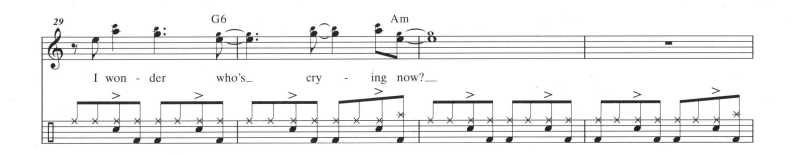

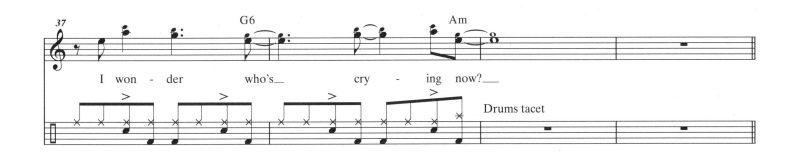

Two hearts born to run. Who'll be the lone - ly one?

I won - der who's cry - ing now? On - ly

Bridge:

so man - y tears you can cry till the

Drums tacet

heart - ache is o - ver; and now you can say your

Interlude:

Band cont. tacet

w/Intro piano cue

love will nev - er die.

Whoa, whoa.

48

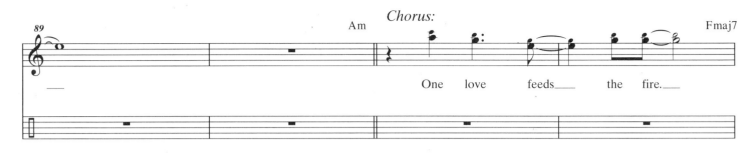

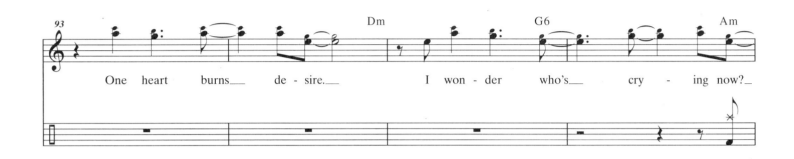

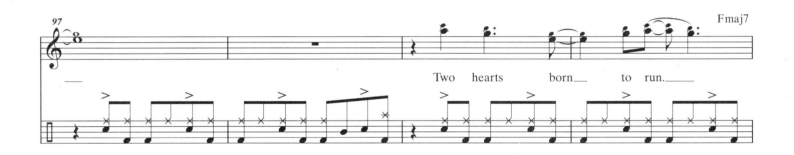

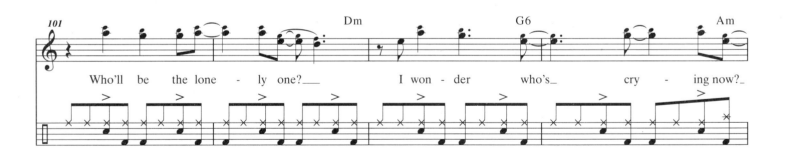

Who's Crying Now - 7 - 5

Drum Charts

DON'T STOP BELIEVIN'

Words and Music by
JONATHAN CAIN, NEAL SCHON
and STEVE PERRY

54

Guitar Solo:

86

90

Chorus:

94

98

102

106

Begin fade

110

Fade out

114

FAITHFULLY

Words and Music by
JONATHAN CAIN

Outro:

LIGHTS

Words and Music by
NEAL SCHON and STEVE PERRY

Guitar Solo:

Chorus:

LOVIN', TOUCHIN', SQUEEZIN'

Words and Music by
NEAL SCHON and STEVE PERRY

Lovin', Touchin', Squeezin' - 3 - 1

Verse 3:

Chorus:

Outro:

63

Lovin', Touchin', Squeezin' - 3 - 3

OPEN ARMS

Words and Music by
JONATHAN CAIN and STEVE PERRY

Pre-chorus:

Chorus:

Drums tacet

SEND HER MY LOVE

Words and Music by
JONATHAN CAIN and STEVE PERRY

Send Her My Love - 3 - 1

Verse 2:

Chorus:

Send Her My Love - 3 - 2

68

Send Her My Love - 3 - 3

SEPARATE WAYS
(WORLDS APART)

Words and Music by
JONATHAN CAIN and STEVE PERRY

Separate Ways (Worlds Apart) - 4 - 1

Chorus:

Verse 2:

Pre-chorus:

Separate Ways (Worlds Apart) - 4 - 2

Chorus:

Guitar Solo:

Chorus:

Separate Ways (Worlds Apart) - 4 - 4

WHO'S CRYING NOW

Words and Music by
JONATHAN CAIN and STEVE PERRY

Begin fade

Fade out

Lights & Faithfully